Untamed Passions

Poems

ALAIN N'DALLA

UNTAMED PASSIONS
POEMS

iUniverse books may be ordered through booksellers or by contacting:

iUniverse
1663 Liberty Drive
Bloomington, IN 47403
www.iuniverse.com
1-800-Authors (1-800-288-4677)

Because of the dynamic nature of the Internet, any web addresses or links contained in this book may have changed since publication and may no longer be valid. The views expressed in this work are solely those of the author and do not necessarily reflect the views of the publisher, and the publisher hereby disclaims any responsibility for them.

Any people depicted in stock imagery provided by Getty Images are models, and such images are being used for illustrative purposes only. Certain stock imagery © Getty Images.

ISBN: 978-1-5320-8191-0 (sc)
ISBN: 978-1-5320-8192-7 (e)

Library of Congress Control Number: 2019914840

Print information available on the last page.

iUniverse rev. date: 09/23/2019

Deep into that darkness peering, long I
stood there wondering, fearing,
Doubting, dreaming dreams no mortal
ever dared to dream before.
—Edgar Allan Poe, "The Raven"

Contents

Preface

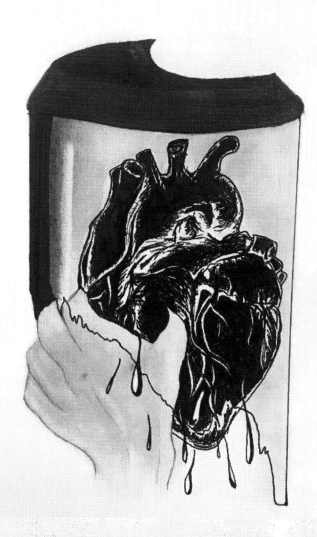

Acknowledgement

to God, who fashioned my brain and its inner workings; who allowed me to think and extract its creativity; who continues to sustian me; who kept me living long enough, and allowed me to publish my debut collection— Dei gratia. Deo gratias. Gloria in excelsis Deo.

to Pascal and Elise, who gave me their all— Ad perpetuam memoriam.

to my muse— my poetic sinoatrial node— Alea iacta est.

to Dwayne, Steven, Seth, Michael, and Tanya who were instrumental in me fostering the pen, and encouraged me to never cease writing my wrongs— Ad majorem Dei gloriam.

to Shauna-kay, who urged me to publish my work— Carpe diem.

to Natasha, who through much sacrifice, helped me to revise and review this manuscript— Fiat voluntas Dei.

to Giselle, whose limitless creativity so ably fashioned the preface according to my vision— Dulcius ex asperis.

to iUniverse, whose exceptional team
made this publication a success—
Calamus gladio fortior.

to my failures, disappointments, and losses that
enervate and galvanize me simultaneously—
Fortis Cadere Cedere Non Potest.

to you, who read this collection—
completely and in its entirety—
Habent sua fata libelli.

Jar of Hearts

I found a jar only slightly ajar,
jam-packed with many a hearts you once stole,
and I took refuge in your abattoir
until my eyes found that lonely buttonhole.
I faintly heard a queer and bizarre thud,
a beating which grew louder and louder,
the air brewing some strange stench of bad blood
as I neared the peak of my encounter.
I pondered a while what my senses sensed,
but the conundrum I could not decode;
then I found that jar and became incensed
when I saw my throbbing heart wince and stowed
in cold blood amongst hearts that beat no more;
I fell prey to Love's terrors and its lore.

Jigsaw Puzzle

Though we have come to naught,
I pick up the pieces,
for I still hunger
for you.
You are my food for thought.

For 'tis the thought that
'twas without a second thought,
that after you, I first sought—
that truly puzzles me.
You are indeed a heavy cross
to word, and
I am bare of a clue to begin with
to fill with ink your crossword.

For I was in for a penny,
and in for a pound of flesh?
Alas, my feelings for you
I found, piece by piece,
but the jigsaw pieces
of my affection failed to live at peace
with yours and mesh.

But on second thought,
why did I not think twice?
A penny for your thoughts?
Perhaps at this crossroads,
it will suffice.

Doctor's Visit

Her stethoscope slithers into her hands,
prepares its assault on my bare chest.
Hair strands shriek as the metal disc lands.
Stranded, my heart prepares its quest.

I look up at her, take a deep breath.
She surrenders, closes her eyes.
Our love did die a natural death.
My heartbeat's bass deafens my cries.

But she hears, and a tear escapes,
falls from my heavy eyes.
My heart surrenders; I eat sour grapes.
Her eyes still glow like fireflies.

Space Shuttle

I hold a stare, looking longingly into space,
bring myself over the moon.
Busy bees break their wild goose chase,
butterflies in their bellies; my stare their honeymoon.

I hold a stare, looking longingly into space,
long enough to see a ghost.
Pale as an unwell undertaker's face—
I look further away, into space's lowermost.

In space's face I find her there,
waiting; we rape our memories to replace
lost time spent flirting with fear.
We gave each other space.

Ring of Roses

Ring a ring o' roses,
A pocket full o' posies.
Atishoo, atishoo, we all fall down.

Like rattle in hand, your hand I held;
you wrung my right hand.
Atishoo, atishoo, I fell.
I still skipped along
whilst you sweetly echoed your song,
now the tale you live
and sing to tell.

Your ring game of folly
nursed my wounds to bleed.
Damn you, nursery rhyme!
Do, dear damsel, depart
lest I wreathe you with wreaths,
throw clocks away, and do time.

For I waddled like a baby,
like a playful child,
like a madman!
Good grief!
You stripped me of my affection
for the sake of brevity;
the rest I tell in brief.

Wring a ring o' roses,
'tis the tune I now softly sing.
squeezing till the nectar cries.
'Tis your tempting thorns
to which I now cling.

Ring a ring o' roses,
A pocket full o' posies.
Atishoo, atishoo, I fall down.

Raincoats in the Sun

We spoke of everything under the sun,
even raincoats.
I was shady; in my tree house we lay.
Sundaes on Sundays—an errand I would run
and ill-treat you at any cost
in my own sweet way.

She spoke of everything under the sun,
even raincoats.
She told her story, and one fable.
She spoke of our chemistry. I led her on,
dined 'neath neon lights,
for me a periodic table.

I spoke of everything under the sun.
Far be it from me to delude her by banter.
I pity my wits for the webs of deceit I spun.
If wishes were horses,
she would unwittingly set off
in the sunset at a canter.

Love at First Sight

Tears handcuff his dimpled cheeks.
She grasps his thumb with her little hand.
He gives strength to her tiny feet,
steadies them until they safely land.

He watches her closely at play
with ladybugs, honeybees, and fireflies.
He holds her hand, teaches her to pray,
points at menacing and blackened skies.

He scans the clock in the waiting room;
from his lips escape a gasp.
He runs ahead to find a sight, sweet as perfume:
she lay there, her hands in prayer clasped.

Tears handcuff his sagging cheeks;
she tightly grasps his feeble hand.
he hurdles each aching step with willing feet.
Finally, he yields and hands her to another man.

Bedtime

Stay the night, my love, in a dream or two,
that I may take your name in vain, my lullaby.
I sleep on it—my dream come true,
and sleep like a baby, rock-a-bye.

Yet, I lure sleep and ensnare fatigue
to hunt for her—a prey I wish not to harm.
Her mind and its ways—a castle of intrigue;
again, I wake to the disquieting sounding of my alarm.

Dreamless sleep, bedtime, nightmare—
all these three spells I fear.
Alas, 'tis a fate worse than death
should you, my love, ne'er be near.

Amusement Park

Absinthe makes your heart grow fonder;
in my sight, out of mind you are.
I swing from your see-sawed emotions;
on my jungle gym you climb each bar.

Higher and higher and higher
I raise the bar; still you climb
till atop you gracefully stand.
Wait for me and poise on a bar's spine.

Fair and square, I come full circle,
my heart an amusement
park you ride, when all's fair in your love
and war, I pay my fare,
take my turn on your slide.

Remembrance of Winter

Winter was kind to me this year,
for my time there with one most fair
sprung a hope unlike any hope I have seen.
In this place, my contemplations have never been.

'Twas her flare that kept my reddened eyes fixed,
like logs of firewood, her eyes burnt constant amidst
the harsh winds that winter found and blew
our way, howling as we whispered a fond adieu.

I remembered that winter long ago,
when our love breasted the blinding snow
and that hope flailed wildly to cushion my fall.
Grasped at nothing, but she stood tall.

Music Box

Locked away in my tiny toy chest
lies my toy story and music box.
I search the rubble, but my eyes find rest
on this thing of music, and I pick its locks.

I wind her up; she fails to play—
to reopen old wounds, perhaps?
A song I long to hear replay:
I toy with her key until it snaps.

That sweet-sounding tune escapes;
she sings again and again her joys
and sorrows, which leave a hollow space
in this my chamber; I burn my toys.

Playing Cards

Oddly stacked against my favour,
I shuffle my own deck, even.
Heart, spade, diamond, and club:
betwixt my seducing fingers they rub.
I lay my cards on your table;
you keep yours up your sleeve.
I succumb to your game of chance;
my own fate I deal.

I batter hearts with clubs;
willingly you follow suit.
A jack of my trade,
I sit confounded and mute.
I call a spade a spade
and a joker but myself,
much ado about nothing,
a comedy of errors
added but to my shelf.

A fake diamond in the rough,
with spades I dig to find.
I draw as I dice with death,
and on your turn you smile behind
cards spread across your face,
a winsome look so unkind.
And on my turn it becomes your turn.
You play a flush with flattery,
within an ace of doom.
I fold prematurely.

Poison

Poisoned by the fangs of uncertainty,
marred and scarred and bleeding internally,
staggered by unfathomable confusion,
was I or am I still in this illusion?

Jets of poison stream through your eyes;
like vision in a blinding blizzard, I fall for your lies.
Choked by deception, injected with pleasant pain.
Powerless I stand, with a perceptible stain.

I sleepwalk in my mind, albeit not sleeping.
Paralysed, I fight your shadowy figure—how relieving!
Haunted by this unrequited love, never fleeting,
I leave your venom to gush through
me and complete its task.
I allow it—willingly?

Pretzel

I never did like pretzels.
Biscuits should be sweet.
You take with a pinch of salt
and think my all deceit?

And words escape our lips—
peace talks after truths.
Bittersweets follow;
we play amateur sleuths.

Salt of my earth,
my pretzel
sweet flower, biscuit.
Salt of my earth,
my pretzel.
Shall I not keep a stick?

Scrapbook

I pass my time pasting pictures,
a pastime I keep till I pass out.
Paste in hand, eyes glued as they land,
unable to find a shorter cut to another route.

For the scraps I collect tell tales,
the other side of our wasted coins.
I toss heads, tails, and think of her,
and feel a stirring in my loins.

Cut up, I bring down our curtain,
scrap the book as the big picture I fail to see.
I tear our pages as my angst rages; beseech
old witches to drown you in the bottom of the sea.

September is the Month

September is the month
that technically follows
July.

When summer school simply
isn't enough.

When parents frown
at another booklist.

When flights are booked less
and people take alternative transport.

When you expect from me
a little more.

When new school shoes' soles shake
at the sight of classroom floors.

When blackboards are bruised by sticks
of chalk to teach another lesson.

When the grass is always green,
and gardeners grow happy.

When an umbrella doesn't wish to spread
its legs and get wet.

Still She Dances

Set to music is her pain,
her abode an opera house.
Her cries crescendo, her sole refrain.
Still, she dances.

Her heart beats to ache;
the conductor still beats time.
Left heartbroken, friends forsake.
Still, she dances.

Many a romantic interlude
for a joy only fleeting,
all wrought but a chase after solitude.
Still, she dances.

Tears tiptoe down her cheeks
mingled with happiness and hurt,
her miserable coda sung by paraquets.
The music stops,
and still, she dances.

The Widower's Song

This sorrow, this sorrow, my bane!
What more shall my tongue confess?
This stain on my heart, this stain.
Oh, teach me to love thee less!

Oh, teach me to love thee less, my love,
my sorrow, my sorrow, my bane!
Shall my tongue confess any less, my love?
Or clouds teach themselves not to rain?

Entreat me to love thee less!
Ah, or take my fledgling heart.
Methinks a dagger upon my breast
a sweet end to tear us apart.

Till Us Do Death Part

There was once a young fair maiden
whom I met in my days of youth.
And alas, on our voyage maiden,
our relationship set sail south.

And my young fair maiden of love did tell,
and that love of all love did come my way.
Like the winds of the north do blow their brief spell,
so did our love reign like the showers of May.

And my young fair maiden of hope did give,
and that hope of all hope in a ray did come
like the frail flower flaunts; her purpose to live.
So did our love boast till our hearts grew numb.

And I thought of my young fair maiden.
I sighed and felt a funeral in my heart.
I laid hope to rest, turned to my young fair maiden,
buried my love; till us do death part.

April 14

Our wreck stays afloat in my sea of emotions,
a relationship sunk for all the world to see.
I wade waist deep in the world's oceans,
drown my raging sorrows in sinking me.

A shipwreck wreaking havoc,
ill-fated like 1912.
The tip of the iceberg we sit,
for April may march again;
the notion of us I slowly shelve.

You took your barefaced bow
a stab in the back; alas, no mean feat.
Now I solemnly stand stern
without a brave front
and vow to ne'er again be swept off my feet.

Spells of Darkness

If I think on you in wake or sleep,
I am no stronger than my sex.
Alas, these things of deep darkness do.
I spell upon myself your hex.

This thing of darkness,
of a truth I perceive naught.
Out, you damned spot!
I wish to wreak you to wreath
my beloved, for 'tis what you wrought.

But when shall we meet again?
On cloud nine in sunshine, or in rain?
Tush, never tell me!
Pinch me to death
'fore I learn of your coming.
Now, go we in content.

Bank Teller Number Three

I bank on our history;
our chemistry I take into account.
Facts flirt with mystery;
I do the math, think straight, rule her out.

I withdraw my hand from hers,
and a bitter, cold draft escapes.
I double-check facts and figures,
and across my mind her figure skates.

She turns and spins her wheel of fortune;
her faint smile puts me on the Ferris.
I try at best to counter her move;
alas, her charm remains a menace.

The Carpenter's Son

He built our house
of pure pine,
built Mother's coffin too.
Many other things he built,
man of the woods, but
never built a home.

I wanted to be like Dad.
"Skilled fool,"
Mother would say.
He didn't hold my hand
as he held his wood
when we crossed the busy street.

I wanted to be like Dad,
learn his trade, build a chair.
One day he put a "for sale" sign
on the front lawn.
We never came back.

The Mathematician

In the aftermath of our love triangle,
I come full circle and eat humble pie.
Angling; scalene—our Bermuda Triangle
unequal; I see doubles; I roll an unfair die.

Alas, my lust goes off on a tangent,
my other half a more vulgar fraction.
In my mind she recurs; no point, absent.
Another significant figure; heat of passion!

Every inch I take—a feat.
I come close and draw a parallel.
We dine at a time table; I take seat.
Second nature, second to none, au naturel!

After the after-effects of our aftermath,
even numbers too count their loss.
She takes the morning-after pill in the afternoon;
afterwards, she counts her loss.

The Flight

In plain view she stood.
My naked eyes craved her more than eyewear.
Then it dawned that she may leave for good.
My eyes climbed up and down a flight of stares.

Alas, my flight was now nigh;
a cloud of doubt hung o'er my mind.
I breathed one last heavy sigh,
then released, for she I did again find.

We were soared above the highest cloud,
a few feet past cloud nine,
far from the madding crowd.
She sat beside me;
today, I do not know her by name.

Portrait of Winter in Nude Apparel

Silhouetted behind her cryptic eyes,
and all the pretences of her inane character,
he is darted with cold, self-inflicted lies,
bemused, confounded by the self-played actor.

Grasped by her icy touch,
frozen by her grip,
paralysed by her poisonous love,
she compels him to slowly sip.

Frostbites of her folly
crunches him to near death.
Weakened by her snowflakes of kisses,
crippled by an aroma from her wintry breath.

Entwined in the envelope of
a long lost dream,
she was Delilah
to silence his scream.

Held captive in the indomitable blizzard,
cold-carpeted air,
hibernation his only option,
for she is a cold, cruel nightmare!

The Funambulist

Tiptoed aloft on a tight, thin thread
amidst where winged seraphs fear to tread.
Arms outstretched, I consider my fall
and walk not the line; an acrobatic jest I stall.

My thrilled audience in patience pre-empts,
but not a finesse finish fathom.
In my stead a silent applause,
a public spectacle; I succumb to the script.

My skilful poise takes wings;
with pride I reluctantly wed
my fate; they in chorus sing—
the funambulist's pleasant requiem.

Scrabble

With her, words oft do fail me, and
my heart knows not the sweet smell of success.
My tongue is left in a labyrinth, lost for words.
Thoughts of the bitter taste of defeat I suppress.

I pick up the threads,
sow the seeds of thought once more.
Clothe my tongue with the very fabric of speech.
Alas, come full circle;
'tis time to settle this score!

I play some more, then scrabble for a foothold.
Mind, soul, and body—all hands on deck.
In words of one syllable, I slip off my tongue.
Now, willing words breathe down my neck.

Ode to the Deaf

Ah, the deaf!
Unable to listen to their hearts,
instead they follow their minds.
Lo, even walls have ears!
They too leave me dumbstruck.
Alas, I take pity on mine.

I wish I were deaf, so to speak;
I could speak my mind then.
For I listen my heart's vain tune,
mute my mind, and act dumb.
I wish I were deaf.
Shall we hear it for them!

Negatives from Your Photograph

I spit on your photograph
perched perilously, leaned against my window,
hanging on a rusty bent nail,
whereupon I ejaculate, twice for pleasure.

Saliva and semen drying,
staining a once fond face—
now a feast for flies.
Familiarity breeds contempt.

Exposed to the elements,
I pray all nature despises you!
As much as you abhor my reflection,
and as much as I do mine too,
I hate myself
for having boldly held your hand
in public and private places.
What a wretched soul I am!

On that window pane you will hang,
crucified by that pitied nail,
on display for all to see
till nature laud my feat.

Hush

I converse with silence,
bid a penny for her thoughts.
In for a penny, in for a pound of violence.
I endure her silent taunts.

In jest, she echoes when I speak;
her food for thought I then ingest.
Silence, time, and I play hide-and-seek.
Time flies like winged insects.

My mind is but a bridge.
Alas, she often crosses it.
My thoughts in full, unabridged.
Silence is golden—
Hush!
For time will tell of it.

Angels and Demons

Cross my heart, hope to love.
Immortal combat—
angels and demons in their course above.
In heavenly realms, their duel plays.
Some favour demons;
on angels some prey.

To those who favour demons,
the fairer sex,
where lie their prey—the dead?
Lesser mortals of love,
if not but in the fury of hell.

And to those who favour angels,
I cross my heart, hope to fly,
then bear witness to a halo figure
embodied in a woman—
wherein fools rush in to die.

A Cursed Curse

Affixed in my depths is the enormity of a curse,
of which potion is poison,
whereof the latter I did nurse.
Whereupon witches bewilder and
all magic laud my feat.
My repulsive charm—
a lethal aroma not sweet.

Twisted like a Rubik's cube,
my mind is distant from thought.
My actions play no act
but are done sooner than said,
rather than sooner said than done.
My dilemma is infinite,
so my death lies not in this reality,
for my solace is but in a dream—
a curse with which the
witches did accurse me.

A Contemplation upon Death

I knew, I knew, that Death was dead certain,
though they mocked his legend, and many were uncertain.
Of fantastic tales that his coming could not be seen or told,
that his face no man could ever in this life behold.

But he pinioned me, grabbed my soul and satchel,
showed me where my body lay in an unfamiliar chapel,
where my kindred sung to me; I heard their wailing cries,
then my spirit slithered past puffy pillows,
into the vastness of the skies.

I inquired of the journey's end, because
from flight we did not rest.
He pointed further into a darkness, then
against an eerie domain we pressed.
And I saw Death, methinks, but I
could not perceive His form.
Then I saw many a kinsmen familiar to
me, through the portal swarm.

Colour My Heart

I was once all alone,
till my hands turned blue with cold.
You offered me a fresh coat
of paint while I stood stoic
by her tombstone.

Then I took of your offer,
became bright like the moody sun,
until you saw my true colours—
when you bruised me;
when you saw me bruise others.

My heart was your canvas,
the paintbrush your penknife.
Little strokes fell great oaks.
Colour my heart some more,
your grievances rife.

Homecoming

I heard Death call out to me today
faintly from the crowd.
Kin and for those I ought to pray,
clad in steam-pressed linen shroud.

He outstretched his hand,
helped me cross the busy street.
Traffic signs and lights he scanned
whose warnings my eyes failed to meet.

I heard Death call out to me today
loudly; he did not hold my hand.
Scolded me, his prodigal son,
in a desolate cul-de-sac.

Winter in the Sahara Desert

Beads of sweat down my brow rock-climb,
survey the sun-scorched sand,
retreat in fear and do their time.
I wander, lonely in a deserted wasteland.

And in the heat of the moment,
a sandstorm brews in our hourglass.
I build you a sandcastle, my atonement
for your inconsistent ways; the worst has past.

But this our drought runs dry;
a fine May day has come.
An oasis of deceit I spy;
to a truthful mirage I succumb.

Neighbourhood Watch

Nestled in unfledged arms, she lies asleep;
seraphs of heaven keep watch while women weep
over empty cradles filled with nothingness,
heralding despair and doubts of just punishments.

And then whoosh! Owls swoop down,
perch upon a mistletoe,
pierce the blackness of the night with eyes that fiercely glow,
forbidding any moonlight to knock and
disturb this sinistrous scene;
women pine away, searching for solace
in a nightmare's dream.

And their wails in consonance echo in the deepest vales,
soar to the highest of heavens to summon imprisoned rains.
Thunderstorms and women, and their aged song,
play a sweet-sounding refrain; I eavesdrop, and erelong
Death steals her from me; alas, I ne'er should
have let her lie in unfledged arms, my
daughter asleep for good.

Remember Me, Amnesia

Fond flashbacks faintly flicker.
I jog my memory down memory lane.
On memory's lane my memories run;
I give chase, but on them I cannot gain.

I burn the candle at both ends
and reminisce; still the past I cannot see.
Nor can I get past the present,
for in its presence I still forget reality.

I sink myself in Amnesia.
She moans in utter delight,
and her name she forgets, for she gets
pure pleasure in my pitied plight.

I thrust deeper, and deeper;
a stroke of luck I receive.
I endure and end your reign in my thoughts,
and now to our past you cleave.

I remind my mind but recall not;
myself, when wronged I forget to forgive.
Amnesia showed me kindness;
a forget-me-not I did not forget to give.

Autumn Springs

In and out of season I fall,
wither whether I stall nature or not.
In the horizon, a menacing squall,
and still I tie the knot.

I bark up the wrong tree;
she sheds her shields until she sticks around.
Left bare to my elements, I lead her to fields
she has ne'er trodden without gown.

Stripped, she seeks closure
to clothe her nudity and fate.
'Fore the cold cannibal strikes,
I play possum and hibernate.

Pen Relays

She raced to her mid-thirties
a little too early,
gave me a piece of her
to keep.
Her pen was delicate,
intricately built—
a fine finish.
I never groped one of these.

I ink my thoughts of her
today and tomorrow.
Will my grasp be set free?
Index, finger, and thumb spar
in a cauldron of lusts,
while her pen still curtsies
for me.

Date in a Hot Air Balloon

I called out to her, but only gently,
and from a deepest slumber she arose.
A weary, weary yawn she did compose,
unlatched her lips to summon my entry.
A form as that of something heavenly
greeted me, and I bore in hand a rose.
An uncertain smile upon her face froze
as she claimed her prize and left me empty.
Then, up and further upwards, in the noon
we surveyed intently the river's course.
Nightfall fell, its wind humming a grim tune,
entreated us to embrace 'neath the moon.
But it's faintest shimmers bred no remorse.
We parted ways in a hot air balloon.

Humpty Dumpty

Humpty Dumpty sat on a wall.
Humpty Dumpty had a great fall ...

I put all my eggs in one basket,
 let them hatch too.
Egg on my ego and mask it
to conceal the yoke of you.

You are but a wild goose chase;
 I'd rather duck hunt a swan.
Birds of a bizarre feather in my nest.
Alas, each of you thwarts my plan.

All the king's horses
And all the king's men
Couldn't put Humpty together again.

Girl at the Bus Stop

My train of thought stopped
dead in its tracks
when the girl at the bus stop
one morning
derailed my habitual morning acts.

Good mornings I rose to see;
alas, the greeting I did not say.
Yet we did set out each morn
walking in contrary way.

My eyes fell on her, followed her
as she cleaved through the crowd.
Her figure drew abreast,
then the wind flung her hair
against my shadow—
our closest and only encounter.

Now, I mourn as each morn dawns.
How unkind is fate a thing to be?
For the girl at the bus stop whom I knew not,
that girl I no longer see.

Untamed Passions

Freshly lit coals lounge in a fireplace
kindled by some strange and constant ember.
Somewhat intrigued by this mystery I face
the distinct, soft crackle bids me venture.
I near its breath that beats upon my brow
to ward some poor stranger unfamiliar
It stokes my anger; its earth I plough,
and a form of some faint and familiar
shadow crawls out from its fiery furnace,
takes us all hostage into its darkness.
The crackling ceases, my passions wordless.
Coals cold; I feel my goosebumps, its sharpness.
Fearing her, I accept without demur,
and she possesses me to play with her.

Picnic

She skipped in the cemetery,
lurid sunflower dress
dancing in the still wind.
Daffodils gazed, green with envy.
A murder of crows flew past,
surveying all who sinned.

She skipped in symmetry,
her feet tapping and tiptoeing
atop thickly grass-covered tombs.
I heard her call out to him today
longingly;
she skipped my funeral too.

She skipped some more,
towards the brook, where
butterflies and caterpillars race.
A duet of laughter disturbed my peace;
they walked a little closer,
sat atop my grave to rest, and
said grace.

Well Played

I tarried as she carefully undressed
her unspeakable affections for him
by a well whose whole grew darker and dim.
And my eyes, straining at the sight, confessed
a chilling truth as her blooded head rest
gracefully in a noose tied at the brim
while stealthy evening shadows veiled the grim
act and its horrors and unwelcomed guest.
I progressed judiciously to the well
that I might perhaps grasp the dreadful deed
and encountered there a revolting smell
as my feet kissed thickets of jimson weed.
The well had swallowed my mademoiselle;
I found her hanging from my neighbour's reed.

Whisky on My Shadow's Breath

I sit and stand by idly,
and watch my shadow—
a bystander standing still.
In a daze, I shift my night,
stand timely, just in the nick,
but against my will.

I stagger, make the last few steps,
lean against a window pane.
Plant a seed of doubt deep
in my shallow depths
and, alas, grow pain.

Still waters run deep,
soiling hopes and burying dreams,
taking an unfamiliar route
to stem the root
of my blooming troubles
by foul or fair means.

Beauty in the Beast

Ah, the beauty I find in this beast
is but a bitter pill to swallow.
She steps up to the plate; my eyes feast.
An eyeful I witness, and tears follow.

Lo, her beauty is not strained;
neither with age can she wither.
With sole purity is she stained.
What wasted work was spent with her!

For still a gaily grim beast she stands,
a wolf cloaked in the wool of sheep.
And bearing sickles as helping hands,
she sows seeds that I still reap.

Comic Relief

I think myself better off today
in a comic strip, or dead.
Infinite fiction like library shelves.
I marvel, and with comic books I wed.

Wherein feelings cannot surface
to fester or by chance infest
the thinker beneath my crooked neck,
where all is foreplay and jest.

Wherein superheroes win
and in a flash fall in love.
I read their end, and
dazzled my eyes become.

Oh, for a king's ransom! Neither Mary,
Jane, nor Lois Lane I would give.
Gratifying my lechery, I drop my eyes,
rest them effortlessly between their cleavages.

I slide my chair beneath the desk,
peer over my shoulders in embarrassment.
In my pocket I place my right hand and
exit the library, whistling some unfamiliar tune,
my bulge the only odd difference.

Water Under the Bridge

We stopped and, abruptly at that crossing,
felt a most chilling parting of the wind.
The scene before us smirked, and her hopes thinned.
I pondered briefly upon this pausing
as the dusk around us kept on falling.
Her feet as clear as mud, soiled and yet trimmed.
To the earth she trudged a long voyage, dimmed
by my volatile ways and recalling
many bridges of old that crossed my path,
that broke as I laboured to bridge our gap.
I fell short, submerged in the aftermath,
many a fall prepared by my own trap.
Water under the bridge. I stirred her wrath
When I made my escape; my bridge I map.

Printed in the United States
By Bookmasters